I0139829

© Copyright 2023 - All rights reserved.

The contents of this book may not be reproduced, duplicated, or transmitted without direct written permission from the author. Under no circumstances will any legal responsibility or blame be held against the publisher for any reparation, damages, or monetary loss due to the information herein, either directly or indirectly.

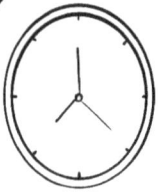

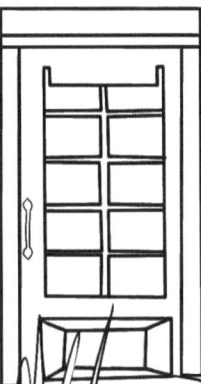

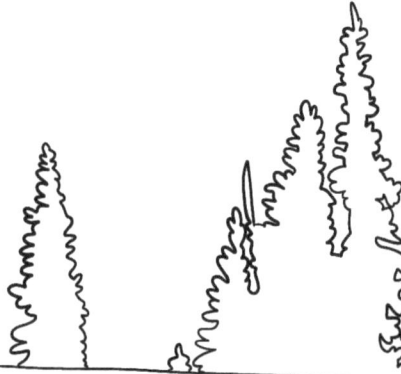

I AM

LOVED

SUMMER LEAGUE: ATHLETES IN TRAINING

SHOP TEAM SUITS

UNSTOPPABLE CAPE

DESIGN CHALLENGE

Design and decorate your superhero cape
then describe your superhero qualities:

_____

_____

UNSTOPPABLE YOU!

Your HERO name

Your HERO features

Draw YOU here

Your HERO superpowers

Unpacking Epilepsy: A Closer Look

```
F  K  L  Y  L  K  M  Q  V  L  A  H  G  S  M
N  E  C  I  H  N  P  F  C  T  O  N  I  C  R
E  H  Z  L  I  Z  P  E  T  R  I  N  R  Z  Q
U  P  W  P  I  L  L  S  F  F  Z  R  P  F  J
R  Z  Y  A  I  M  E  D  I  C  A  T  I  O  N
O  R  C  R  N  G  W  U  W  E  R  Y  O  F  E
L  V  U  D  M  T  J  V  R  I  I  I  B  P  S
O  B  R  T  I  F  T  S  E  I  Z  U  R  E  N
G  H  E  E  D  O  C  T  O  R  U  J  F  D  V
I  B  E  H  A  V  I  O  R  H  M  C  E  A  B
S  Q  X  A  B  S  E  N  C  E  B  F  G  N  M
T  U  N  O  A  P  Q  F  A  U  R  A  B  R  K
Y  E  S  D  A  I  F  F  I  R  S  T  A  I  D
V  Q  P  E  P  I  L  E  P  S  Y  Z  N  H  I
X  K  S  P  J  N  M  A  H  N  R  R  S  C  G
```

EPILEPSY	CURE	BEHAVIOR	MEDICATION
FIRSTAID	DOCTOR	PILLS	TONIC
NEUROLOGIST	SEIZURE	AURA	ABSENCE

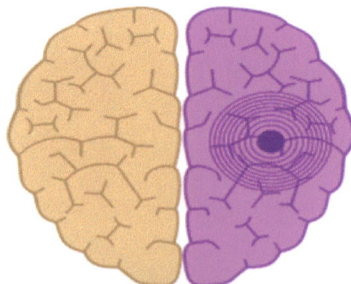

I AM LOVED

Name: _____

Superpowers: _____

Unstoppable Me

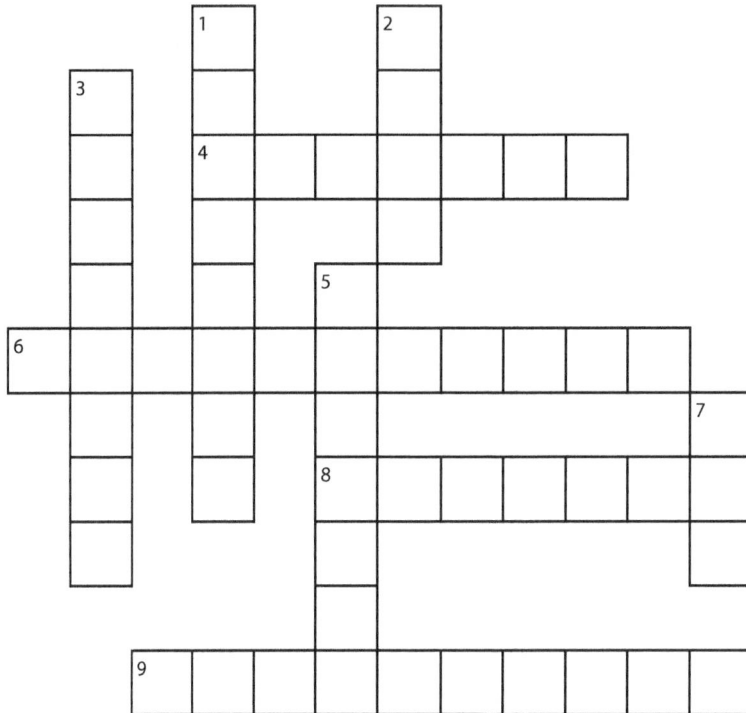

Down:
1. therapist
2. strong
3. benign
5. aura
7. IEP

Across:
4. rest
6. epilepsy
8. neurology
9. brave

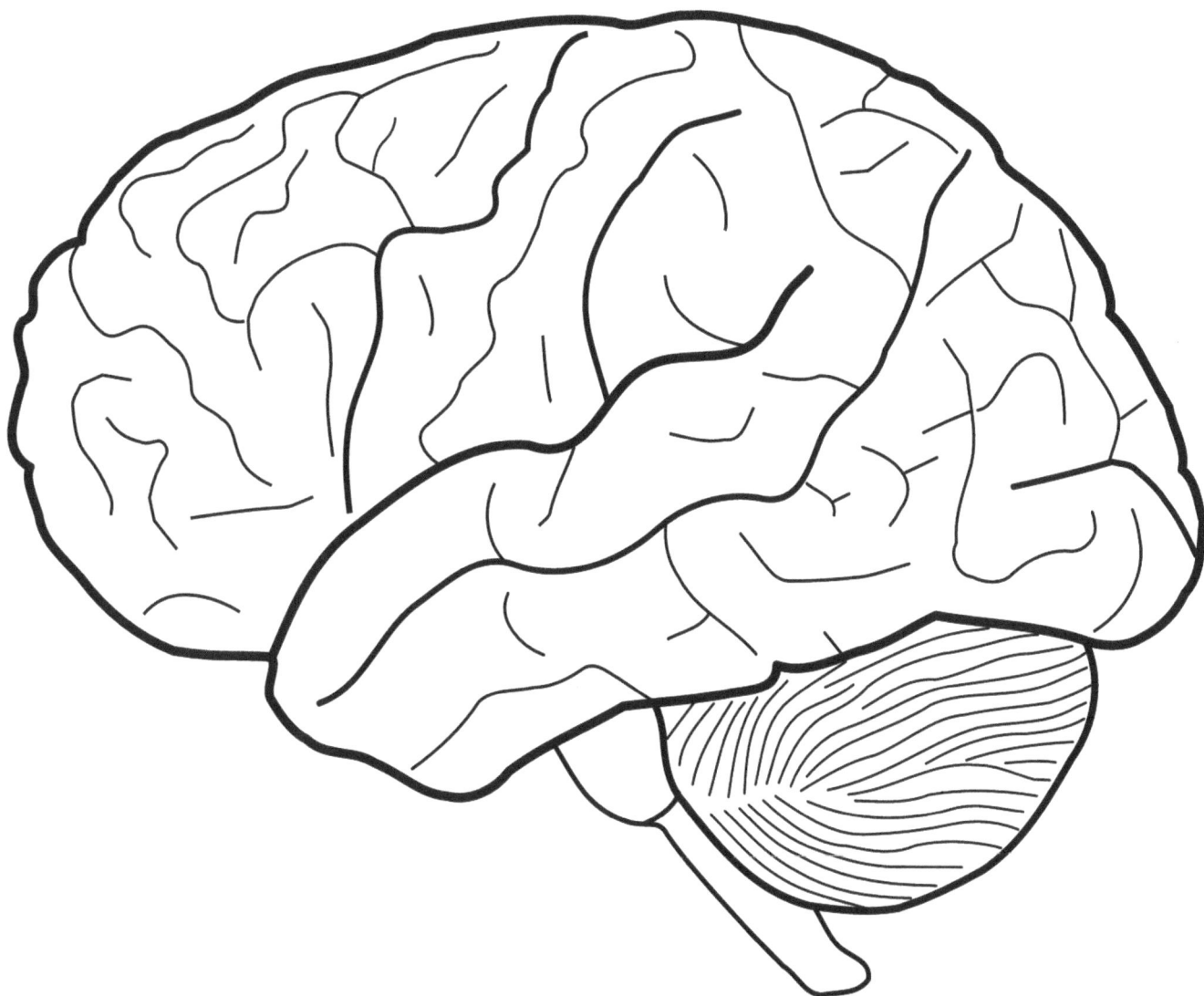

BRAIN

The first word describe you

A	L	S	M	A	R	T	O
K	I	N	D	M	A	R	H
H	A	P	C	A	C	U	A
C	U	T	U	Z	O	S	P
A	R	E	T	I	R	T	P
F	R	I	E	N	D	L	Y
A	S	N	A	G	O	O	D
L	E	A	F	U	N	N	Y
C	R	E	A	T	I	V	E

Make lemonade out of the lemons in your life...

Thank you...!

www.ingramcontent.com/pod-product-compliance
Lightning Source LLC
Chambersburg PA
CBHW041428090426
42741CB00002B/87